Pebble® Plus

What Makes a Family?
Family Traditions

by Martha E. H. Rustad

PEBBLE
a capstone imprint

Pebble Plus is published by Pebble
1710 Roe Crest Drive,
North Mankato, Minnesota 56003
www.mycapstone.com

Library of Congress Cataloging-in-Publication Data
Library of Congress Cataloging-in-Publication Data is available on the Library of Congress website.
ISBN 978-1-9771-0907-1 (library binding)
ISBN 978-1-9771-1050-3 (paperback)
ISBN 978-1-9771-1277-4 (eBook PDF)

Editorial Credits
Marissa Kirkman, editor; Cynthia Della-Rovere, designer;
Eric Gohl, media researcher; Tori Abraham, production specialist

Image Credits
Alamy: PhotosIndia.com LLC, 13; AP Photo: Jim Mone, 7; iStockphoto: kali9, 9; Shutterstock: Andy Dean Photography, 1, DGLimages, 17, Halfpoint, 19, Jacob Lund, 5, Mila Supinskaya Glashchenko, 15, wavebreakmedia, 21, Wong Yu Liang, cover, ZouZou, 11
Design Elements: Shutterstock

All internet sites appearing in back matter were available and accurate when this book was sent to press

Note to Parents and Teachers
The What Makes a Family? set supports national standards related to social studies. This book describes and illustrates traditions families share. The images support early readers in understanding the text. The repetition of words and phrases helps early readers learn new words. This book also introduces early readers to subject-specific vocabulary words, which are defined in the Glossary section. Early readers may need assistance to read some words and to use the Table of Contents, Glossary, Read More, Internet Sites, Critical Thinking Questions, and Index sections of the book.

Printed and bound in China.
001654

Table of Contents

What Is a Tradition?

A tradition is done over and over for a special reason. Adults teach traditions to kids. Families pass down traditions about food, clothes, and fun.

Food

Asin's family gathers wild rice. His grandpa taught his mom this family tradition. Now Asin's mom takes him in the canoe.

Rosa's family has a birthday tradition. They hang a piñata. It is filled with candy and treats. They fall out when it breaks! Kids rush to pick them up.

Abdi's family has an afternoon tradition. They take a tea break. His grandma makes tea. It is sweet and warm. They eat cookies with their tea.

Clothes

Kalima wears traditional clothes for special days. She wears a dress called a sari for a wedding. She loves the colorful sparkles. They dance to music.

Wearing a hijab is a tradition for some women. Isra wears a scarf over her hair. She likes the bright colors. Isra asks her sister for help with her hijab.

Family Time!

Maria's family has a holiday tradition. Her family surprises a friend. They sing Christmas songs at her house. The friend shares her food with them.

Hila's family has a morning tradition. They say a special prayer. Hila's grandma taught Hila the words. Hila gives thanks for the new day.

Soren's family has a bedtime tradition. Mom reads Soren's favorite book. His dad sings a song. This family tradition is a way to show their love.

Glossary

canoe—a small, shallow boat that people move through water with paddles

grandma—the mother of a person's mother or father

grandpa—the father of a person's mother or father

hijab—a veil or head scarf sometimes worn by Muslim women and girls

piñata—a hollow, decorated container filled with candy or toys; a person tries to break the piñata with a stick.

prayer—a set of words meant to give thanks to or ask for help from God

sari—a long piece of cloth that is wrapped around a woman or girl's body

sister—a female sibling

tradition—a custom, idea, or belief that families pass down through time from adults to kids

Read More

Amstutz, Lisa J. *Applesauce Day*. Chicago: Albert Whitman & Company, 2017.

Penfold, Alexandra. *All Are Welcome*. New York: Alfred A. Knopf, 2018.

Steinkraus, Kyla. *Holidays and Traditions*. Really Weird, Totally True Facts About. Vero Beach, FL: Rourke Educational Media, 2017.

Internet Sites

Christmas in Puerto Rico
https://www.whychristmas.com/cultures/puerto_rico.shtml

Harvesting and Processing Wild Rice
http://www.native-art-in-canada.com/wildrice.html

National Geographic Kids: Thanksgiving Traditions
https://kids.nationalgeographic.com/explore/history/thanksgiving-traditions/

Critical Thinking Questions

1. What is a tradition? How do traditions get passed down in a family?

2. What is your favorite holiday tradition?

3. Do you have any daily or weekly traditions?

Index